The Man Who Takes Care of My Soul

A second collection of poetry

Sigari Luckwell

Inquiries and Book Orders should be addressed to:

Great Writers Media
Email: info@greatwritersmedia.com
Phone: 877-600-5469

ISBN: 978-1-959493-78-5 (sc)

When the man who takes care of your soul, knocks on the door of your heart and invites you to dance, what will you do?"

To the universal in us all

Contents

Foreword

This is Sigari's second volume of poems to which I'm happy once again to write a brief foreword. Like those of her first volume they are very personal, deeply felt and sometimes raw. As she says in her introduction, she wants you to hear her voice, to imagine her speaking the poems to you. This is easy for me, since I've heard her speaking her poems, which she does directly and from the heart.

Perhaps because I know Sigari from holidays in the Lake District, I associate her with William Wordsworth, whose house in Grasmere I have visited with her. She shares with him and focus on what he calls 'spots of time', moments in which he felt a close connection to nature or to people, moments of intense feeling which nourish the soul through more difficult or more prosaic times.

Like Wordsworth, Sigari focuses on seemingly small events, little acts of kindness or of contact with other people, small pleasures such as the eating of ice-cream or the sharing of a poem. It is by treasuring these moments, she claims, looking at the world with the wonder of a child,

that we are able to 'create our own souls' and to preserve
them in the wake of the inevitable disappointments and
difficulties of life.

There is also a vein of protest running through the poems,
protest at the way we treat each other, other nations and
the planet. Sigari will often challenge you personally with
a direct question, asking what you would do in the same
circumstances.

So these poems are not altogether comfortable reading.
You will be made to question your assumptions and to think
how the world might be made a better place. But I can
promise you one thing: you will not be bored.

Terry Wright.
Emeritus Professor of English Literature
Newcastle upon Tyne, England

Preface

When I was very young the man who takes care of my soul knocked on the door of my heart and invited me to dance. It was the occasion of my fifth birthday at home in Ickenham near London. There were eight or nine other children, most of them girls and three boys. The party was in full swing and we had eaten cake, jelly and ice-cream to the full. My mother shepherded us out of the dining room and into the lounge where we were free to play. She went into the kitchen and began washing up. We started playing a game about a newspaper office. I was the editor and other friends were journalists, photographers, type-setters, layout artists and the like. How, as five year olds we knew all about these jobs I cannot say, but we did and entered into the game with great gusto. We played at meetings where stories were discussed, 'photographs' poured-over and decisions about final design were made. It was enormous fun. In the middle of it, my mother opened the door and came in to pick up stray cups and plates to wash. She walked into the game completely unobtrusively and we played on around her. I was sitting in the armchair near the fireplace facing the French windows leading out to the back garden. My mother leaned over, picked up a cup on the table next to me, and then stood up and walked off. In the moment she leaned over, something inside me exploded or imploded. I merged with everything and everyone around me. It was a sense of disappearing and yet life and the game continued. I felt ecstatic and as if all boundaries had gone. In the same way, it was all very ordinary and I could see that everything was just happening; there was no doer or doers in it. To say I merged or I was aware is not strictly true; there was no I to merge, though I did not have the words for that at the time. There was also a sense of knowing what was going on everywhere all at once or even what was about to happen, much like a global 'deja-vue.' This sensation of being merged with all lasted some time throughout the rest of the party and a while after. I felt joyously happy for seemingly no reason.

I never mentioned this experience to anyone at the time or for many decades to come. It did not seem to have been 'caused' by any prior event, though I vividly remembered my mother leaning over me and the game we were playing as triggers for my young mind. The following year at my sixth birthday party I wondered if that 'thing' would happen again. As my friends arrived, I felt it to some extent; a joy, an expansiveness, but nothing like what had taken place the previous year.

Each year since I have invariably throw a big birthday party and played games. Or I have lead workshops and meditations much like the editor in charge of a newspaper run by five year olds. Such are the ways of the mind when it comes to trying to recreate the circumstances of longed-for happenings!

Since then, there have been other glimpses, but the power of my five year old experience and the intense awareness it brought were fundamental. The book of poems you hold contains rough diamonds, not exquisitely honed but diamonds none the less. They were written from that space of merging which has visited me from time to time at certain moments of life's own choosing. I commit them to publication for your enjoyment and as a way of keeping them recorded. Thirty two new poems are presented here for your enjoyment, since the publication of the first volume three years ago.

Please read these poems slowly, perhaps to each other with a friend. Take your time and savour them bit by bit. It is always second best to read them from the page: a few are now on Youtube but otherwise, please, imagine my speaking them to you, one heart to another.

Sigari Buckwell
October 2016

Acknowledgements

My sincere thanks to those who helped with editing formatting, presentation and style:

* *Maneesha James, (writer and editor) for her brilliant insights and editorial comments.;*

* *Catherine Martin and Holly Luckwell for their help in editing, style and presentation;*

* *Two poets, Norm Flynn and Dosh Luckwell contributed much in editing and poetic formation.*

I am very grateful to Tony Martin for his tireless help in all areas, especially formatting the presentation of the final manuscript
All your inputs have helped enormously with presenting material on paper; a task I often find difficult in translating the spoken word into the written word..

Much gratitude goes to Jerry Wright for his beautiful Foreword and the opportunity to share some of these poems in person with him, and his wife Gabby.

I also wish to express my gratitude to Osho for his understanding of the true power of words for change and new life in a world where power is more frequently acknowledged through destruction

A thank you also to those who respond at Open Mic Nights and Poetry Slams and other events, with your praise, criticism and encouragement: it is always good to hear that you have been touched by a piece of poetry. I enjoy the support we can all give each other at these word events.

The Man who Takes Care of My Soul

When the soul makes contact, do we listen? This poem has been performed at various venues in Australia and also in the UK. You can google it as a You Tube clip (Sigari Luckwell Poetry) being performed at Rich Mix in Shoreditch, London in September 2014.

*****

When I was very young, the man who takes care of my soul knocked on the door of my heart and invited me to dance.

It was so exciting!
I jumped up and we tumbled out into the sun and the rain to play, while crystals of colour made a rainbow and eternity passed.
Then the school-bell rang.
I had to learn that two and two made four;
how to ride my bike; how to dress;
how to deal with the bully in the yard at recess.
I had to learn running writing and how to shut up
when grown-ups were talking, sipping tea from a cup.
So I told him to go away.

He gave me his calling-card and he left.

When I was a young woman, the man who takes care of my soul
knocked on the door of my heart and invited me to dance.
But I was busy!
There were people to love, some to be near;
others to leave; and then, my career.
There was even sport and he didn't look the sporty sort.
By then there were children, I mean, couldn't he tell?
Life was too full for his visits as well.
And why not a woman? Why was he a man?
My female mind rankled; I had other plans.
I had mountains to climb; new things to try;
errands to run, I don't know why.

So I told him to go away.
Away he went without a word.
From him again I never heard.

Over the years he would sometimes come to mind.
His calling card was, I knew, just behind
all my stationery, near an old pen.
I'd kept his card, 'cos that's what you do.
You keep calling cards that people give you,
even when there's no intent to ever, ever meet again.

One day in a deep and darkened hole
I rang the man who takes care of my soul.
Yes, there was a number and he appeared!
He looked just the same, not aged as I feared.
He didn't knock on the door of my heart or invite me to dance.
We eyed one another and I knew at a glance.
I'd spent years avoiding this man and my soul.

Would he still help me now in my bid to be whole?
"I'm sorry," I said, "that I sent you away
when all that you wished was to dance and to play.
I know I've betrayed you; been deaf to your whispers.
It pulls at my heart-strings which lie here in splinters."

He didn't respond and I stood there quite lost -
words useless and futile - just counting the cost.
I looked at him closely, consumed in my shame.
He gazed at me steadily with no hint of blame.
And then, drawn in by the light in his eye
I saw that it twinkled and I started to cry.
Then I looked deeper still and saw in that light
the dance of the spheres lifting me from my night.
It wasn't a question of him or my life in the world,
but of two beating hearts that together unfurled.

When the man who takes care of your soul knocks on the door of
your heart and asks you to dance, what will you do?

Heavenly Shower

It wasn't clear which button to press or squeeze or pull or turn.
The sign said CAUTION very hot: I did not want to burn.
A turn was made, like grace from heaven, sweet warmth did touch my skin.
Droplets flooded with gentleness, my body moved right in.

The shower was perfect, full yet soft - I sang its praises loud.
The founder of this bathing place, they really should be proud.
No royal queen could wish for more, no empress or princess
than this humble bathroom's gifts that had no need to impress.

I stayed at least five minutes or six relishing every drop.
The water stayed hot/warm/hot warm and *never* once did stop.
Where are we now? 'for I forget and this bliss grows old and dim; at the Warwick Racecourse Caravan Club; birth-place of this hymn.

Page 5 Will Do

Do you realise how much power you have?
I am sure you do.
I plead with you to use it wisely.
Instead of fraud and futile violence,
ring the bell for a moment's silence.
And as for the murder, page 5 will do.

Our sales will fall, I hear you cry.
'Good news don't sell,
the reader wants hell.!'
A disgusting choice for what's truly human.
That's not a solution,
it's mind pollution- choose love.

Don't listen to the mind's desire
for excited news
or distorted truths.
You can *help* the world to drop sensation.
Is it a hopeless task,
too much to ask,
to change a sick, perverted fascination.?

You *should* inform, not hide what's true
but leave the gory detail be.
I challenge all you members of the press;
to those of you who feed our minds
to leave the garbage far behind- choose love.

A headline shocks - a heart-line's needed.
Instead of all this useless chatter
let's talk about the things that matter.
Drop this collective body of pain.
It strikes and somewhere deep within
promotes a debasing, numbing din- choose love.

Are we not yet fed up enough
with feeble-minded acts
and sordid facts?
Why sift among the dross and mud
when diamonds shine
and what is fine-is love.

Do you realise how your power could be harnessed for gold?
I am not sure you do.
With tomorrow's headline from an enlightened press,
you can lighten this dark, darkening night
and stem the rotten, hype-filled blight.
Become a beacon of consciousness.
and as for politics- page 5 will do.

Sacred Surprise

I had a text from God today
brief and quite surprising.
'A parcel will arrive at noon
The angel will deliver soon.'
Now that was most enticing!

But midday came and midday went
No sign of any sacred gift.
Perhaps the angel lost its wings
or got caught up with other things.
My hopes were dashed - I was bereft.

I read the text once more right through
In case the date was somehow wrong.
But as before it read the same
It even started with my name
And still, for something did I long.

And just as I could bear no more
For sweetness to my heart was pressed.
The object simply fell away
And while the yearning, it did stay
It now was longing *unaddressed*.

The gift was there in God's first text.
With limitlessness all around,
I'd looked outside; it was *inside*
Doors now were open; what a ride
And gratefulness, it did abound.

The angel then appeared and said
''Got the message! Time has no reversal.
Start anywhere but sing your song.
The words and tune will come along;
For of life there's no rehearsal.'

From Paralysis to Bliss

I'm numb when the newscaster talks of airstrikes in Iran.
I'm numb when scientists say the Arctic ice is disappearing.
I'd like to roar,
but can't 'cos I'm raw,
and we must keep the economy from nearing a crash
and making us poor.
So, no rocking the boat and let it keep us God-fearing.

I'm numb when a heinous crime is mentioned in the news.
I'm numb, though might manage to say, 'how sad'.
I'd like to roar,
but can't 'cos I'm raw
and we must stop the economy going bad, or giving us more.
Either way, paralysis stops us going mad.

I'm numb but I'm comfy thank you very, very much.
I'm numb and......I'd like to let it go.
I'd like to roar
just a little bit more,
even when feeling raw,
or hurt and sore.
But I need to take it really, really slow
And what it will do to the economy, I do not know.

So I move my hand from the remote to yours.
Our fingers press, we pause
Let me look into your eyes,
allowing uncertainty and surprise.
I honestly want to give up the familiar.
Now I tingle and my breath is deeper,
I look and your heart meets mine.
There's no better space on earth than this
(far better than paralysis).
I want nothing from you
Well, that's not strictly true.
All I ask is,
Let's remind each other of this;
Follow your bliss, follow your bliss.

As Within So Without

As without, so within.
You must have heard the *If only, then, but* poem; probably
many times.
If only there were peace,
then all peoples would love one another. *But.*
If only there were peace?!
Have you looked inside yet?
What do you see?

I see the clap-trap of mediocrity
and a freeway of thinking
incessant blinking
as the mind cavorts
with sharp retorts;
a cesspool truly stinking.
No, that's not peace.
Not peace at all.
It's war;
inner gore.
What for?
Please no more.
But resisting it?
That's not peace either.

For there's a fight
of inner might.
It isn't right
to shut out light.
Let's see this mess as it is,
exposed and raw.

How to deal with our dark
when there's no inner spark
And no sign coming down from above?
We have to learn how
'cos the time's only now
and the planet's in need of some love.

There's spark there alright
But it just wants to fight
And destroy and to smash and annihilate.
And while reason says no
it's a million decibels below
and of wisdom it wants to procrastinate.

For I know about ire,
that it often makes fire
but destroys all in its path as it does so.
There must be a way
to turn it and play
with the energy staying in vivo.

And sometimes it's needed:
let the warrior be heeded,
as we meet a hellish dark wretch.
What relief to hit out;
say what's never been said.

Not to worry what's politically correct.

Let's not make it a pattern
of cause and effect;
that just leads into depths of disaster
Once or twice is enough
when the going's been tough,
but we don't want to end up in plaster.

In the thick of the moment
anger looks like a mountain
as if only murder will lessen the rage.
That's how the mind does it;
to keep up old patterns.
We can turn a new leaf… or a page.

Oh I so so so so
wish it could be so.
I'm concerned we sow
And reap old, ancient habits
that are so-so.

A scream from the boots
at that very peak moment
when the ire explodes at its worst.
Leave granny's delicate china
Hit out and punch at the air
Nothing: no-one that's precious need burst.

The ego won't like it
and tell you that's silly.
It wants much more drama than that.

But the truth is that's plenty
to let ourselves empty
of ire from its molten, hot vat.

That fire we can harness
For good or for ill
And we see how that's played out in wars.
If we want peace out there
We must find it inside
It won't come from diplomacy's doors.
The clouds when they're parted leave no room for doubt
Let warmth be compassion, for as within, so without.

The Deep End

Small private moments take place in the most unlikely of places.
While participating in an Aquatherapy class I could not help but
see the caring exchange between these two people outside the pool.
Are we not witness to countless moments like these; life is always
providing them?

*****

Who did I notice first?
The nearly vacant stare of the black-haired young woman
or the strong, blond, tanned back of the carer
who lifted her carefully onto the wheelchair,
as if her charge were the most precious being in the world?

A little later I looked over
to see the carer lift the young, black-haired woman's legs;
lift them high and shake them,
before lowering them gently on and over the edge of the chair.
Of course!
To free the muscles of the buttocks and thighs
from any awkward positioning when seated for a long time.
What thoughtfulness;
learned through experience.

Some time passed before I looked again
and caught a magic moment.
Ministrations were done
and a beautiful shawl completed the moment.
The black-haired woman, whose stare was not so vacant after all
looked up at her carer.
"Thank you", she said.
"You're welcome", was the reply.

A jewel of an interchange - all two seconds - which struck a chord
in my heart.
Tears streamed down my face as I turned away.
Tears flowed into the pool;
tears of gratitude for witnessing the grateful exchange.
Did anyone else notice?
I don't know.
There were eleven of us there.

Later gentle eyes were on our backs.
I turned right around in the water.
The two were relaxing, after the physical negotiations of the
wheelchair,
watching our antics in the water.
The strong blond carer met my gaze.
We smiled instantly, broadly, at each other;
her smile like the sun, sparkling and wide.
As my eyes travelled back to class, they glanced briefly at the
young woman
whose stare was now half vacant.

Suddenly the mother appeared; black-haired.
Aha, They were waiting for her!

Final, last-minute adjustments;
putting on the young woman's glasses.
Then, time to go and they left through the door.

"Now ladies, take a noodle each and let's go to the deep end!"
The deep end?
I'd already been there twice in the last fifteen minutes.

Aging

The Beatles made a legend about turning sixty four
Their words were 'many years from now'
But look, behold the door!
It seems absurd to contemplate that we are growing older
When feeling much more like a child that sees the world
with wonder.

I'm not quite sure what aging is but, as the years go higher,
tennis is not punchy as it was some decades prior.
The body has its journey, which I notice every day;
a slow capitulation into frailty and decay.
The mind is just hilarious and stacks on quite a show,
Forgetting keys and glasses and 'Where is it I need to go?'
It's hard to take it seriously when I feel so free and light
And as this form dissolves it's really, truly, out of sight.

I'd like to say I've lived My Way, but that's not quite correct,
For early on and still today, there's a button called auto-select.
A mother's words, a father's moods - they all have had their place
And the exorcism continues, leaving more and more pure space.

A still small voice can just be heard above the raging din
and seems to guide an exploration more and more within.

You know, that prompt beyond the mind that says a quiet 'Yes,'
to some unknown adventure with a yet unknown address.
And even when it's saying 'No, I won't go out tonight.'
It's really always more a 'Yes' to what's inside and right.
And then it takes me by surprise; instead of suggesting resting,
It wants me on the dance floor, skipping high with life and zesting.

And like a flower moving from a budding bud to blossom
It starts to be more clear to me, the present day life's lesson.
The outer bloom begins to wane, though still giving of its scent
and radiance from beyond shines through more easy; translucent.
Life seems more full
Less full of bull
And somewhere there's an inner pull.
Yet somehow life, it still needs me and still feeds me as I age
and move toward a mystery and onto a new page.

Alarmingly Responsible

I saw a different way to go
(I was alarmingly responsible)
and penned it 30 years ago
while crying in the night.
Vision not wanting sight.

These are the words that were sung then
(I was alarmingly responsible.)
Will it suffice to sing again?
No harm in telling you
what in my heart was true.

'Look all around you, the world it is dying
a hundred new species a day.
What's close to our hearts is now close to extinction,
there must be a different way.
So open your eyes and then close them
sing with your heart open wide.
I don't know the answers perhaps they'll come later,
just look at the treasure inside.'

Then in my prime I truly thought
(I was alarmingly responsible)

that other's hearts I could exhort;
to stop and love the earth
and share our inner worth.

I read the news today, it said,
(Am I alarmingly responsible?)
the planet is as good as dead.
I just curled up inside
and wished that I could hide.

Only for so long can you dread.
(Are we alarmingly responsible?)
From activism to staying in bed,
my being then went numb;
like others, I'll play dumb.

I'm not so sure now of the way
no longer seeing what is possible.
It's not enough to sing and pray,
but use me as you will;
let's take this bitter pill,
for we're alarmingly responsible.

Innocent Eyes

The plight of those we see as 'other' grows as a global issue as asylum seekers look for somewhere safe to live. This poem grew out of the personal experience of needing a roof for a short while and understanding the needs for containment and privacy that stop us opening doors and hearts. This poem has been performed at the Dardanup Bull'n Barrel festival in Western Ausralia and various Open Mic Nights. It won a Poetry Slam in Exeter this year and was performed at Rich Mix, in Shoreditch, London in July this year. It has always been well received and can be viewed on You Tube (Sigari Luckwell Poetry).

*****

Innocent eyes, looking straight at me with a story to tell.
Would you like to hear it? Do you really want to hear it?
I'm not sure I can bear it anymore, so I turn off the TV.
What a relief.
No more grief.
Not now.

But that night she looked at me again on the dream screen of my mind.
Sleep was no escape; she found me there and told me her story.

I cried, *we* cried at the rape of her mother; the pain, anger and frozen years since.

She laughed *(laughed)* with such hysterical fervour at the murder of her brother, it made my skin crawl and wince.

Yet her eyes were innocent.

"I just want a home," she said.

For forty days and forty nights we have bobbed upon the ocean, looking for the promised-land.

I just want a home."

So because it was my dream, and why not, I invited her in.

And there was no-one to ask for a visa or passport: no-one with an official stamp, no forms to fill in or interviews to be endured.

She was overjoyed and we started dancing, the kind of dance that gives your boots wings and lifts your arms heavenward to fly.

It was ecstatic yet so simple, so ordinary; and afterwards we sat and laughed.

Would I be so welcoming in the light of day?

She might take over my precious space and fill the house with the smell of too much spice as she cooked dinner.

She might be awkward in social situations and embarrass me.

And what if she talked loudly and invited all the relations in?

What would I do? What would you do?

What if she cut up the bed-linen to make clothes for her family, or started growing weird-looking vegetables I had never heard of before, in the garden?

And what if they all worked so hard, I felt guilty?

Maybe I am a coward.

I *think* I want freedom for all, a place for all, peace for all, but do I really?

Then I remember the warmth of friends who took me in when my children were small and I had no home.

A large sunny lounge; I was so grateful.

Next, I slept under another friend's massage table, while my children slept on blankets in the same room as her children.

Then next, in a friend's sleep-out where the cold sweat from the foam mattress soaked me night after night.

I did not stay long; three weeks at most.

Was it an eternity for them?

On each departure they cried. Can you believe it? *They* cried.

"Why must you go?"

I left because the living force for individuation resides in all beings, just as it lives in those asylum seekers.

They just want a chance to find their feet.

The danger is we might learn to love them while they are here, to open our hearts once more and know what community really means.

I am willing to take that risk.

There is no passport office in my heart.

Don't Speak To Me

The young and very young men and God forbid, perhaps even young women who are groomed to inflict terror on others, do so out of misguided conditioning from their elders. This poem is directed at those 'teachers.' How shocking to see this in ourselves as they mirror this violence back to us. Can we learn from it? Can we stop polluting young, fresh minds? This poem has received strong recognition at Open Mic Nights.

*****

Don't speak to me of sacrifice, of a noble and glorious death.
Don't speak to me of honour for a cause.
And give us back the innocence of young men in their prime,
That they may live for something other than wars.

Don't speak to me of martyrdom and virgins up in heaven.
Don't speak to me of justice and of hate.
And give us back those fit young men with passion in their souls,
that they may love this life before too late.

Don't speak to me of self-spilt blood absolving all past sins,
Don't fill their minds with rubbish and with guilt
And then lay on redemption and the path to full atonement

and talk forgiveness when blood's first drop is spilt.

Don't speak to me of lust for power, revenge and domination.
Stop telling these young minds of higher goals.
Don't speak to me of making fear to overcome corruption;
that their God's sweet revenge will save their souls.

Don't speak to me of training them for suicide and terror.
Don't tell me they are queueing for their chance
to die for God who rewards them later on.
Give them back so they may learn to dance.

Your teaching is an abomination, more so than what they do.
I will seek help and expose its poisonous pus.
I will not rest until beliefs and rotten history, are gone,
letting what is truly human shine through each of us.

And finally, I salute your cowardice and your rotten depravity.
How else would I see the coward who lurks within the heart of me?

Let Your Little Light Shine

There is a light in each of us that shines for all to see,
but sometimes it gets covered up and blocks out you from me.
If only we would understand, there is no need to fight;
another's flame does not compete, it simply throws more light.

The final shot at Wimbledon, the trophy is held high.
The loser's heart is heavy and the winner's heart doth fly.
If only they would understand, the game of tennis won;
that each of them has played their part and added to the song.

Just as the actor takes his bow whether hero or the villain;
the play's success has needed *all* front and backstage men
and women.
No worthwhile venture ever shone on just one mortal soul:
life cries out for us to participate and contribute to this whole.

For we are not all separate: that old ego illusion,
which maintains such one-upmanship and keeps us in confusion.
For letting your light shine is an important public duty,
not for fame and riches but to enhance life's daily beauty.

The Poet of Dublin

A brief meeting in a Dublin city mall in 2014: one of those precious moments with an earnest young poet.

*****

Streetdancers;
moving prancers;
accomplished guitarists;
a man with a clever scream
as I ate my Irish Whiskey ice-cream.

"D'ya like my poem, will ya fill ma cup."
I was reading the words, no time to look up.
"Let me get to the end" I said.
He turned to make another friend.

The words they were painful, striking and raw:
I could tell he meant it, that he felt very sore.
The last line was light as I coined his cup;
"I'm glad your pain is better" and with that he looked up.

"Thank you", he said as we talked on in words
of the need to express and the need to be heard.

His face it was scarred but his heart it was true;
"It helps with my pain if I share it with you".

We parted as friends, he said, "Colin's my name".
Only *my* coins in his cup, but maybe the flame
in his poet's heart doesn't care about that,
as he wrote with his chalk and I stopped for a chat.

Age 90

When I wrote this poem, my uncle loved it (he also loved ice-cream!) and would recite it to himself at night in order to help with falling asleep. He died earlier this year age 97: this poem is in rememberance of him.

*****

If I reach the age of ninety,
I just want to know in advance,
that there's money enough for a daily ice-cream
and a place I can visit to dance.
No need for a large house or boat
or even a fancy fur coat.
I won't need a Jag or a Merc or a Rolls
n'less we come across a cheap one by chance.

If I reach the age of ninety,
I just want to know for sure,
that there's money enough for a daily ice-cream
and water to drink that is pure.
No need for much overseas travel,
enough, to not slip on the gravel,
and teeth that will manage a good hearty bite

of an apple right down to its core.

If I reach the age of ninety,
it won't matter to me who's in power,
long as there's money enough for a daily ice-cream
and to be stunned by the sight of a flower.
No need to go partying each night,
'nough to read and be able to write.
I won't need gourmet meals
or meals on wheels;
just enjoying the moment or hour.

If I reach the age of ninety,
I will wander around in a dream
and be counting my pennies to know there's enough
for a daily and creamy ice-cream.

Did You Doodle?

When my Father died in 2011, I inherited his pen.

*****

The mystics are like untrained scientists with a deep sense of awe.
They say every action, every thought, leaves a vibration.
Every garment, piece of jewellery worn, or implement used, by someone,
leaves a trace;
a soul print.

The other day I picked up my father's pen;
 a much used pen in his time.
Would I feel anything of this man of letters?
Maybe the vibrations changed after each penning, depending on whether he was:
signing a cheque,
tallying up the month's budget,
addressing many Christmas cards,
doing the Times crossword,
writing a love letter,
making a shopping list,
writing a letter to the newspaper,

sketching the plan for a treehouse on a napkin,
penning a poem or a note to a friend.

Did you doodle?
If only I could ask him.
I suspect your doodles were scrunched up and thrown in the bin;
though sometimes your legacy left scribbles which became
fine drawings
and they have been kept.
At first, my words with your pen were spiky and small
but already I am training it to write with bigger, rounder letters,
and I am writing more.

My father who art not here,
hallo-ed be thy name (RJVS)
This pen be filled;
these words be writ,
on paper as it were in the heart and fist.
And let us script beautifully,
as we would delight in those who scribble wisdom, beauty and
nonsense for us.
And lead us not always to the computer screen,
for thine is the quill, the ink, and the parchment,
for ever and ever,
Amen.

God Has Only You

We have to create our own souls. It's not God given.

It *is* actually.
If we would just get out of the way and allow the spark to
be bestowed.
Then we can create the soul.
This freedom is a responsibility
we can rise to meet or cower in its quest.

Words fail me but I must find my own.
We must all find our own song:
throw off the songs of others
and stand naked before God.
My daughter did that with her first fashion collection at university.
"The naked courage to be oneself", she said.
"Such that everyone is beautiful as they are."
For the truth is, God has only you to work with.
You are the eyes of the divine, the ears and the voice:
it chooses *you* as its instrument, let *it* be your choice.

Chocolate Understanding

Today's salad plate
was all that I ate,
and it's no big deal
to miss the odd meal.
I've been so good
with my bowls of food.
So could we please come to a little chocolate understanding?

I've been for a walk,
I can walk the talk.
Even rode my bike;
something I quite like,
and when times are rough,
I still have just enough.
But could we please come to a little chocolate understanding?

I've no self –control,
just lucky on the whole;
no real issue with weight
or what's on my plate.

Surely you can tell
that I've done quite well.
So could we please come to a little chocolate understanding?

How's Your Love Life?

How's your love life?
The words rang out clear, even sing-song in her quietly Danish way.
The voice, my mother's dearest friend,
warm buddy to the very end.
Behold this greeting; this late night invitation to play.

The tone is hers, its own sweet song as if she's sitting here with me.
It could no other be than her,
no need to doubt, guess or infer.
A voice so real it would invoke her face for me to see.

She never asked about a job or where I lived,
nor touched upon philosophy, religion or the arts.
She steered away from business, taxes, even education,
much preferring the joys of love and matters of the heart.

No political or financial news would ever make her tick.
No time for duty, obligation,
royal honours or reputation.
No messing about, her question cut down to the quick.
How's your love life?

But it isn't easy when these whispers come at night,
full of notions and wakefulness in the wee small hours.
I wish not to disturb him or turn on any light,
as next to me his dark shape sleeps and quietly towers.

So I have a spiral notebook by the bed
and can feel the edges firm enough to write,
and the words spill into dark from deep inside my head
and in the morning my writing looks a dreadful sight.

That's how I know I love him.
When there's no need to disturb him and I can still be me.
How's your love life?

Sun Worship

We arrived late in the UK summer just as autumn had begun, having left a budding Spring behind in Australia.

*****

I left Australia just last week where spring has just begun;
new budding shoots are everywhere and the birds are having fun.
A bronze-wing pigeon fans its tail and bows in hopeful greeting;
his feathers splashing gold and green, with hopes for a consummate meeting.
She runs away, he follows of course,
again and again and again.
A ritual cycle of instinct and lust
that looks to be almost in vain.
Once, he jumps, maybe twice in a dance that is long.
She's finally stopped her endless escape
and they find a brief moment of love-song.

And now I'm here, you've had your sun and are readying for its waning.
My body objects, 'hey we'd just gotten going!' its music has turned to complaining.

Were you to visit Australia right now, it would not be the same sort of feeling:
two rounds of sun, why yum, yum yum, you'd be soaking it up, you'd be reeling.

The sun gives us life and Vitamin D especially if baring your trunk.
Its golden light that its rays emanate, oft leaves us feeling quite drunk.
And given my age or this stage in my life, an autumn is much too appropriate.
Whereas new summer and spring bring the promise of zing, an exuberance that's new, to procreate (or at least redecorate).

Let's give thanks to the sun and its live-giving warmth whether spring or summer or autumn.
For even when bleak, it lights up our lives and of enlightenment brings a small portent.
For our light is inside and the mystics all know that when all is said and is done,
Our souls will awaken and the light of that grace will shine like thousands of suns.

Handle With Prayer

Which Bible shall I read today,
what scripture take to heart?
I long for understanding,
to know of life, what is my part?

Sometimes the words of Jesus
seem to sing a song of love.
Another day and Buddha
shines a light of grace above.

I search the words of Bodhidharma
or the life of Mahavir:
the dancing flute of Krishna
and the poems of Kabir.

And all those Vedas seem to do
is just increase my thirst.
Inside their words there is no truth;
no treasure in there first.

The gemstone seems to lie elsewhere;
in nature and its realm;
a child's smile, a flowering rose

without me at the helm.

So of my heart's small offering;
Fragile, lacking intellectual flair,
I ask you to use some sensitivity
and handle it with prayer.

Bright Here Waiting

I'm bright here waiting,
Contemplating;
what will happen next?
(For Brext)
The pound's gone down.
Will it turn around?
Oh, here's another text.
No cause for laughter,
it's my daughter
saying they're sad and shocked.
They can't believe it;
the country's hard hit,
and from the world will they be mocked?
(or trade blocked?)

Circus Suit

On his arrival in London to start a new life we took my son to Oxford Circus to buy a suit. Thousands of shoppers there created a chaotic energy. A smart suit was purchased but with further trying on that night, it was obviously too small (just). Next morning it became clear there was no option but to return and make an exchange.

*****

The heart sank, willing it not to be so
But, there he was.
A smart man: a very smart man.
Don't look too closely.
We needs must
For around the bust
It's tight.
Too tight for real comfort and movement;
too tight for future work in a new life.
We needs must return
to yesterday's circus.

Sleep

I'm lying here quite wide-awake.
Hast thou forgot our meeting?
I wait upon our heavenly date
when we rejoice in greeting.

My thoughts are tumbling to and fro
my body quite at rest.
Indeed lights flit around my eyes
A radiance of zest.

Perhaps our dates are ending soon
or won't last quite as long.
Are we to loosen life-long ties
as I begin my song?

Poem for Cynthia

Goodbye beloved Cynthia, mother of my dear friend Maneesha.
After four days of them holidaying with us before New Year,
Cynthia returned home and died a few days later. After 97 years
of a full life we celebrated her death, enhanced by Maneesha's
understanding and love with imparting conscious living and dying.

*****

"Did you throw the ball for Bindi?
Did she run and bring it back?"
asked Cynthia with a twinkling eye
as through the flyscreen she'd espied
us returning from a walk.

"Of course I did, not once, not twice,
but more and more and more.'
And Cynthia stroked her doggy friend
and laughed and laughed when I complained,
"and now my arms are sore."

"Did I mention my bridge partner?
whose marriage now is broken?

I don't *think* that it was due to me"
with just a hint of mischievous glee
as thus her words were spoken.

If I were there come even time
through TV programs she would scan.
She really liked to watch QI
and not because of Stephen Fry
but Alan Davies was her man.

And never was it difficult
to know the time for leaving
She'd suddenly say, "You can go."
She'd had enough of me and lo
with her blunt words I'd go laughing.

And just a couple of years ago
at a Death Café in Bunbury,
I partnered Cynthia for a game
in which we had to sort and name
our wishes for dying comfortably.

We looked each other in the eye
until I thought we'd melt
I can't remember a thing she said;
not a single word stays in my head,
but I remember how we felt.

For what is that beyond the mind
beyond all deeds and thoughts
that place of pure consciousness
where peace lies under any mess
that's claiming shoulds and oughts.

Thank you Cynthia for your smile and laugh
your sharp and ready wit
beloved family members I met
Your gorgeous, exhausting canine pet.
For being with me in it.

Yarloop

Last summer the township of Yarloop in Western Australia was burned to the ground in a bushfire. Within seven minutes, 121 homes were gone. There are doubts about the town's survival as a community.

*****

Yarloop.
Is God teasing it?
Really.
Better to have burned completely.
Better still, not burned at all.
For now a shell is all that lingers
that, and a hazy, smoky pall.
Meanwhile the politicians promise relief funding; that's all crap,
to give hope; a consolation for the future, a real mind-trap.
They *say* that kind of thing after an event that's tragic
As if pouring in the money makes the community magic.
And while it certainly helps: if not just words,
Will it also help with wildlife, fences, herds?
For after such a trauma it takes time to regrow.
We know the flora will return and bloom again
the insects, birds and fauna will return, we know.

And will the humans? Will the women, children, men?

We hear the cries of those who mourn
where many lived, died, were born.
Those in Yarloop in its dark hour
stood and watched as flaming power
destroyed the very thing they shared,
a place where people loved and cared.
These broken hearts will build anew:
they want their town to live and grow
Are they many?
Are they few?
Are they enough?

We hear the cries of those who doubt
saying Yarloop will come to nowt.
We've thought this town a blemish for some years
with its symptomatic sicknesses and tears;
bleeding noses, headaches, cancer, they're all noted;
yes, history of timber-mill and steam are doubtless quoted.
But it's time to move on now and start anew.
No-one's going to have the oomph to grow what here once grew.
And besides we've wanted here and Hamel out the way
So the refinery can grow and have its say.

If you really want to know what will happen to Yarloop's township
Listen to the people who've lost homes; who've suffered hardship.
Take each one by the hand and look deep into their eyes,
ask 'do you want your community to live or to die'?
They may not know.
Can you give them space not to know?
as meanwhile, a new kind of community grows,
as helping hands reach out with food and clothing for those lost,

and new friends give beds, cars, babysitting with no thought for cost.

And some may stay and some may go;
there is no right and wrong.
as each moves on their inner flow
and we listen to Yarloop's song.

The only thing we know for sure
is that we are alive. But are we?
Are we too in limbo?
To choose each moment life or death
for our brief moments here on earth
Which way will we go?
Don't ask will Yarloop rise or fall,
that's not what's relevant at all
But how much life will we know?

Will we die to trust or open up
Even to the heart that breaks?
That in the breaking of the heart
There comes about a deeper space.
A space so new, so collective that we see only sister and brother,
where individual goals abate and we learn love for one another.
Here endeth Yarloop's lesson.
Thank you Yarloop.

Gratitude is Orange

Bright orange, golden yellow flames are licking, leaping from the trees.
Words can't express the fear and fascination,
of men and women dressed to fight, who
battle the odds of *their* incarceration.
As the inferno rages day and night,
this orange army of liberation,
the same colour as their foe,
work with such deliberation
to save wildlife, our lives from woe.
An army of collaboration
Bent on peace
Soldiers of restoration,
while nature throws its next challenge at the crumbling world.
They've come from near and far to join the firefighters.
Gratitude is orange.

Glen Ridding

We spoke with some men at Glen Ridding
who were building a new wall in town.
In a flood last December the old one came down
'Build in 22 weeks! You are kidding!'

And these workers recalled at Glen Ridding
when of sustenance they were deprived,
how a lorry of Muslims arrived
bringing food and drink just for their bidding.

And the world could learn much from Glen Ridding
where a community opened its heart
and trusted each other rather than honing the art
of just fighting and constantly quibbling.

The Fisherman
of Craster

Today I did speak with a fisherman from Craster
who don't go to sea anymore.
Each morning at 7 his personal guidance from heaven
sends him down to the fish-cleaning floor.
For seven hours they split and they bone and they strip
all the fish for the markets out your way.
And today I did learn a ton a day comes through here
with herring that's caught up in Norway.
The kippers of Craster are coming through faster
and keeping us in our consumer bubble.
But while herring's still flowing;
let's be true to our knowing
that red ones can lead us to trouble.
The North Sea is dying, the fish have run out
That's no cause for cheers or celebration.
The fisherman must earn his bread.
Does Jesus' miracle lie ahead
of the fishes and loaves, or just procrastination?

The Haddenham Macaw

Sitting in a garden in Buckinghamshire we were surprised to see a brightly coloured macaw land high in a tree next door. We learned later he had escaped from the local fish and chip shop (not for the first time). How strange must it have been to inhabit a new land far from his original home. I was reminded of my own escape many years before when leaving home with a child and the strange new life it catapulted me into.

*****

So we were privy to his escape
as he soared high aloft.
His heart, I wished that I could soothe;
it touched me tender, soft.

For, thirty years ago today,
my aching soul took flight.
One child in hand, one in the belly;
hard, pioneering plight.

I'd left my cage and all I knew.
No trace was left behind
and everything in life was new.
Where are those of like kind?

My raft was gone, no welcoming shore
or even a shore I'd left.
New birth ahead and challenges more:
times were difficult and bereft.

And even the new as it knocked at my door
was so new, that it made my heart ache.
From riches to rags I now was quite poor:
a tumultuous inner earthquake.

I could no more go back, that was clearly the case
and while scared, I at least now, was free.
Though life then erupted with explosions of grace
It was basically children and me.

My trust was just budding: it was still far too soon,
to know, existence would cradle me soft:
that there would be others to sing with and laugh,
to help me in flying aloft.

So I wondered aloud as the macaw flew on by
As we heard he'd escaped just that day,
if his colourful presence and grating macaw call
in a land of brown birds, showed the way.

Lady Spinner

This was written as a song in July 1989. Our lives are like a tapestry that we weave. At some stage even that story has to be left behind as we leave behind the world of the mind and step into the beyond.

*****

Lady Spinner, casting out my fate,
lace gold and silver threads into the weave.
Fill up my life with beauty and with truth
And let goodness be the final tapestry.

Lady Spinner, you give me what I ask.
Won't there be pain and retribution from above.
If I receive whate'er my heart desires,
How will that teach me self from selfless love?

Lady spinner, I see you smiling there
with fingers trailing threads of shining gold.
Behind us blows that lovely tapestry,
as you and I in laughing tears dissolve.

Lady Spinner, takes me by the hand
and like a bubble floats into the sky.
I say goodbye to a cherished world of old
and facing upward spread my wings to fly.

Lady Spinner, thank you for your gifts;
Dreams and imagination played their part.
This wondrous path we've travelled far along.
You knew this end would be but a new start.

These Stones on Which You Sit Tonight

This poem was written for an annual music concert held at the Amohitheatre just outside Harvey (a town in Western Australia) and was performed in the summer of 20i4. While it's story is of the local area, the poem is written from the point of view of the stones which have acted as a witness to history over millennia.

*****

These stones on which you sit tonight have watched lives come
and go and wish to tell you something of their story:
how they're hewn from local quarries,
trucked by endless loads of lorries
and have ended up as Amphitheatre glory.

These stones once lived as river beds in old Triassic time, over 250
million years ago.
From core they now are crust
why, some are fertilizer dust;
yet others are moving back and going down below.

The Noongar peoples knew these stones and loved them at their source;
and for 40,000 years they were great friends.
Such majesty was sung
and even writ upon
a place to go and pray and make amends.

These stones saw May Gibbs arriving here as girl of only eight: the family came in 1885;
No schooling meant Mum taught her
Dad's artistic talent found his daughter
And the rest is Snugglepot and Cuddlepie.

And the dam of stones surrounding us is the final one of three: the first constructed during WW1
They used men with horse and dray
Can you imagine that today?
And the heat and flies were no-one's idea of fun.

It held 500 million litres and that lasted for a while: then in 1931 they built some more:
The walls went up to 18 metres
Holding over 2,000 million litres,
They'd never seen one quite as big as that before!

And as Harvey life expanded, the need for water grew: the final dam brought forward fourteen years!
That's astounding news to ponder,
And creates a sense of wonder
for we're so used to budget cuts, delays and fears.

This edifice was finally finished just a dozen years ago, storing so much water, that the figures make you dizzy,

Just to count the daily flow
as it cycles high and low
must keep lots of number-crunchers really busy.

Geologists are working hard to tap the Lesueur basin and sampling
deep from underneath these rocks
To deal with SW industry waste
3km cores they have taken in haste
So that hereunder can be a CO_2 storage box!

So as you watch and as you listen, take a moment to reflect and
maybe to feel the stones upon which you now sit;
for they've borne witness to the show
of universal come and go
and they know how just to be and say, "this is it".

Will the Last Person to leave the Planet......

Will the last person to leave the planet please blow out the candle?
Buddha may be there and ask, 'Where does the flame go?'
It'll blow your mind as he pares all away to nothing.
While good in his day, these ways can be hard to handle.
He deals in negatives and speaks of 'neti-neti,'
'not this-not that,' a big emptiness
that fails to convey the fullness of nothing.
Methinks, not suited to the 21st century.

If you meet Jesus, he may still be fuming about the money lenders.
Tell him the greedy businessmen have gone; no need to curse.
Get him to chill out a bit: lovely bloke.
He'll show you where the stepping stones are to the rest of
the universe.
He's more of an extravert: more a man of action.
Actually--- no, no no, there won't be a second coming.
I mean, would you? if your last visit ended in crucifixion?

If you see Osho, you are in real trouble!
Best to kill him first as he'll be doing the same to you.

Will the last person to leave the planet please feed my cat?
His name is Schrodinger and he may, or may not, be in the box
on the mat.

www.ingramcontent.com/pod-product-compliance
Lightning Source LLC
Chambersburg PA
CBHW031230120626
46545CB00003B/1068